This **MAN** in **MOTION!**

A Man's Daily Planner

ACTIVINOTES

Activinotes

DAILY JOURNALS, PLANNERS, NOTEBOOKS AND OTHER BLANK BOOKS

A Daily Planner

DATE: _____

THINGS TO DO:

Schedule

time	task

- _____ ☐
- _____ ☐
- _____ ☐
- _____ ☐
- _____ ☐
- _____ ☐
- _____ ☐
- _____ ☐
- _____ ☐
- _____ ☐
- _____ ☐
- _____ ☐
- _____ ☐
- _____ ☐
- _____ ☐
- _____ ☐
- _____ ☐
- _____ ☐
- _____ ☐
- _____ ☐
- _____ ☐
- _____ ☐
- _____ ☐

COMMENTS: _____

A Daily Planner

DATE:

THINGS TO DO:

Schedule

time	task

COMMENTS: _____

A Daily Planner

DATE:

THINGS TO DO:

Schedule

time	task

COMMENTS: _____

A Daily Planner

DATE:

THINGS TO DO:

Schedule

time	task

COMMENTS: _____

A Daily Planner

DATE: _____

THINGS TO DO:

Schedule

time	task

_____ ☐
_____ ☐
_____ ☐
_____ ☐
_____ ☐
_____ ☐
_____ ☐
_____ ☐
_____ ☐
_____ ☐
_____ ☐
_____ ☐
_____ ☐
_____ ☐
_____ ☐
_____ ☐
_____ ☐
_____ ☐
_____ ☐
_____ ☐
_____ ☐
_____ ☐

COMMENTS: _____

A Daily Planner

DATE:

THINGS TO DO:

Schedule

time	task

COMMENTS: _____

A Daily Planner

DATE:

THINGS TO DO:

Schedule

time	task

☐
☐
☐
☐
☐
☐
☐
☐
☐
☐
☐
☐
☐
☐
☐
☐
☐
☐
☐
☐
☐
☐

COMMENTS: _____

A Daily Planner

DATE:

THINGS TO DO:

Schedule

time	task

COMMENTS: _____

A Daily Planner

DATE:

THINGS TO DO:

Schedule

time	task

☐
☐
☐
☐
☐
☐
☐
☐
☐
☐
☐
☐
☐
☐
☐
☐
☐
☐
☐
☐
☐

COMMENTS: _____

A Daily Planner

DATE:

THINGS TO DO:

Schedule

time	task

COMMENTS: _____

A Daily Planner

DATE:

THINGS TO DO:

Schedule

time	task

COMMENTS:

A Daily Planner

DATE:

THINGS TO DO:

Schedule

time	task

COMMENTS: _____

A Daily Planner

DATE:

THINGS TO DO:

Schedule

time	task

COMMENTS: _____

A Daily Planner

DATE:

THINGS TO DO:

Schedule

time	task

COMMENTS: _____

A Daily Planner

DATE: _____

THINGS TO DO:

Schedule

time	task

_____ ☐
_____ ☐
_____ ☐
_____ ☐
_____ ☐
_____ ☐
_____ ☐
_____ ☐
_____ ☐
_____ ☐
_____ ☐
_____ ☐
_____ ☐
_____ ☐
_____ ☐
_____ ☐
_____ ☐
_____ ☐
_____ ☐
_____ ☐

COMMENTS: _____

A Daily Planner

DATE:

THINGS TO DO:

Schedule

time	task

COMMENTS: _____

A Daily Planner

DATE:

Schedule

time	task

THINGS TO DO:

☐
☐
☐
☐
☐
☐
☐
☐
☐
☐
☐
☐
☐
☐
☐
☐
☐
☐
☐
☐
☐
☐

COMMENTS:

A Daily Planner

DATE:

THINGS TO DO:

Schedule

time	task

COMMENTS:

A Daily Planner

DATE: _____

THINGS TO DO:

Schedule

time	task

- ☐ _____
- ☐ _____
- ☐ _____
- ☐ _____
- ☐ _____
- ☐ _____
- ☐ _____
- ☐ _____
- ☐ _____
- ☐ _____
- ☐ _____
- ☐ _____
- ☐ _____
- ☐ _____
- ☐ _____
- ☐ _____
- ☐ _____
- ☐ _____
- ☐ _____
- ☐ _____
- ☐ _____
- ☐ _____
- ☐ _____
- ☐ _____

COMMENTS: _____

A Daily Planner

DATE:

THINGS TO DO:

Schedule

time	task

COMMENTS: _____

A Daily Planner

DATE: _____

THINGS TO DO:

Schedule

time	task

- _____ ☐
- _____ ☐
- _____ ☐
- _____ ☐
- _____ ☐
- _____ ☐
- _____ ☐
- _____ ☐
- _____ ☐
- _____ ☐
- _____ ☐
- _____ ☐
- _____ ☐
- _____ ☐
- _____ ☐
- _____ ☐
- _____ ☐
- _____ ☐
- _____ ☐
- _____ ☐
- _____ ☐
- _____ ☐
- _____ ☐
- _____ ☐
- _____ ☐

COMMENTS: _____

A Daily Planner

DATE: _____

THINGS TO DO:

Schedule

time	task

COMMENTS: _____

A Daily Planner

DATE:

THINGS TO DO:

Schedule

time	task

☐
☐
☐
☐
☐
☐
☐
☐
☐
☐
☐
☐
☐
☐
☐
☐
☐
☐
☐
☐

COMMENTS:

A Daily Planner

DATE:

THINGS TO DO:

Schedule

time	task

COMMENTS: _____

A Daily Planner

DATE:

THINGS TO DO:

Schedule

time	task

COMMENTS: _____

A Daily Planner

DATE:

THINGS TO DO:

Schedule

time	task

COMMENTS: _____

A Daily PLANNer

DATE: _____

THINGS TO DO:

Schedule

time	task

- ☐ _____
- ☐ _____
- ☐ _____
- ☐ _____
- ☐ _____
- ☐ _____
- ☐ _____
- ☐ _____
- ☐ _____
- ☐ _____
- ☐ _____
- ☐ _____
- ☐ _____
- ☐ _____
- ☐ _____
- ☐ _____
- ☐ _____
- ☐ _____
- ☐ _____
- ☐ _____
- ☐ _____
- ☐ _____

COMMENTS: _____

A Daily Planner

DATE:

THINGS TO DO:

Schedule

time	task

COMMENTS: _____

A Daily Planner

DATE:

THINGS TO DO:

Schedule

time	task

COMMENTS: _____

A Daily Planner

DATE:

THINGS TO DO:

Schedule

time	task

☐
☐
☐
☐
☐
☐
☐
☐
☐
☐
☐
☐
☐
☐
☐
☐
☐
☐
☐
☐
☐
☐

COMMENTS: _____

A Daily Planner

DATE:

THINGS TO DO:

Schedule

time	task

COMMENTS:

A Daily Planner

DATE:

THINGS TO DO:

Schedule

time	task

COMMENTS:

A Daily Planner

DATE:

THINGS TO DO:

Schedule

time	task

COMMENTS: _____

A Daily Planner

DATE:

THINGS TO DO:

Schedule

time	task

☐
☐
☐
☐
☐
☐
☐
☐
☐
☐
☐
☐
☐
☐
☐
☐
☐
☐
☐
☐
☐
☐

COMMENTS: _____

A Daily Planner

DATE:

THINGS TO DO:

Schedule

time	task

COMMENTS:

A Daily Planner

DATE:

THINGS TO DO:

Schedule

time	task

COMMENTS: _____

A Daily Planner

DATE:

THINGS TO DO:

Schedule

time	task

COMMENTS:

A Daily Planner

DATE:

THINGS TO DO:

Schedule

time	task

☐
☐
☐
☐
☐
☐
☐
☐
☐
☐
☐
☐
☐
☐
☐
☐
☐
☐
☐
☐
☐
☐

COMMENTS: _____

A Daily Planner

DATE:

THINGS TO DO:

Schedule

time	task

□
□
□
□
□
□
□
□
□
□
□
□
□
□
□
□
□
□
□
□
□
□

COMMENTS:

A Daily Planner

DATE:

THINGS TO DO:

Schedule

time	task

COMMENTS: _____

A Daily Planner

DATE:

THINGS TO DO:

Schedule

time	task

COMMENTS: _____

A Daily Planner

DATE:

THINGS TO DO:

Schedule

time	task

☐

☐

☐

☐

☐

☐

☐

☐

☐

☐

☐

☐

☐

☐

☐

☐

☐

☐

☐

☐

☐

COMMENTS: _____

A Daily Planner

DATE:

Schedule

time	task

THINGS TO DO:

- ☐ _____
- ☐ _____
- ☐ _____
- ☐ _____
- ☐ _____
- ☐ _____
- ☐ _____
- ☐ _____
- ☐ _____
- ☐ _____
- ☐ _____
- ☐ _____
- ☐ _____
- ☐ _____
- ☐ _____
- ☐ _____
- ☐ _____
- ☐ _____
- ☐ _____
- ☐ _____
- ☐ _____
- ☐ _____

COMMENTS: _____

A Daily Planner

DATE:

THINGS TO DO:

Schedule

time	task

COMMENTS: _____

A Daily Planner

DATE:

THINGS TO DO:

Schedule

time	task

☐
☐
☐
☐
☐
☐
☐
☐
☐
☐
☐
☐
☐
☐
☐
☐
☐
☐
☐
☐
☐

COMMENTS: _____

A Daily Planner

DATE:

THINGS TO DO:

Schedule

time	task

COMMENTS: _____

A Daily Planner

DATE:

THINGS TO DO:

Schedule

time	task

COMMENTS:

A Daily Planner

DATE:

THINGS TO DO:

Schedule

time	task

COMMENTS: _____

A Daily Planner

DATE:

THINGS TO DO:

Schedule

time	task

COMMENTS: _____

A Daily Planner

DATE:

THINGS TO DO:

Schedule

time	task

COMMENTS: _____

A Daily Planner

DATE:

THINGS TO DO:

Schedule

time	task

COMMENTS:

A Daily Planner

DATE:

THINGS TO DO:

Schedule

time	task

COMMENTS: _____

A Daily Planner

DATE:

Schedule

time	task

THINGS TO DO:

☐
☐
☐
☐
☐
☐
☐
☐
☐
☐
☐
☐
☐
☐
☐
☐
☐
☐
☐
☐
☐

COMMENTS: _____

A Daily PLANNer

DATE:

THINGS TO DO:

Schedule

time	task

COMMENTS: _____

A Daily Planner

DATE:

THINGS TO DO:

Schedule

time	task

☐
☐
☐
☐
☐
☐
☐
☐
☐
☐
☐
☐
☐
☐
☐
☐
☐
☐

COMMENTS:

A Daily Planner

DATE:

THINGS TO DO:

Schedule

time	task

COMMENTS: _____

A Daily Planner

DATE:

Schedule

time	task

THINGS TO DO:

- ☐ _____
- ☐ _____
- ☐ _____
- ☐ _____
- ☐ _____
- ☐ _____
- ☐ _____
- ☐ _____
- ☐ _____
- ☐ _____
- ☐ _____
- ☐ _____
- ☐ _____
- ☐ _____
- ☐ _____
- ☐ _____
- ☐ _____
- ☐ _____
- ☐ _____
- ☐ _____
- ☐ _____
- ☐ _____
- ☐ _____

COMMENTS: _____

A Daily Planner

DATE:

THINGS TO DO:

Schedule

time	task

COMMENTS: _____

A Daily Planner

DATE: _____

THINGS TO DO:

Schedule

time	task

- _____ ☐
- _____ ☐
- _____ ☐
- _____ ☐
- _____ ☐
- _____ ☐
- _____ ☐
- _____ ☐
- _____ ☐
- _____ ☐
- _____ ☐
- _____ ☐
- _____ ☐
- _____ ☐
- _____ ☐
- _____ ☐
- _____ ☐
- _____ ☐
- _____ ☐
- _____ ☐
- _____ ☐

COMMENTS: _____

A Daily PLanNer

DATE:

THINGS TO DO:

Schedule

time	task

COMMENTS:

A Daily Planner

DATE:

THINGS TO DO:

Schedule

time	task

COMMENTS: _____

A Daily Planner

DATE:

THINGS TO DO:

Schedule

time	task

COMMENTS: _____

A Daily Planner

DATE:

THINGS TO DO:

Schedule

time	task

COMMENTS:

A Daily Planner

DATE:

THINGS TO DO:

Schedule

time	task

COMMENTS: _____

A Daily Planner

DATE:

THINGS TO DO:

Schedule

time	task

COMMENTS: _____

A Daily Planner

DATE:

THINGS TO DO:

Schedule

time	task

☐
☐
☐
☐
☐
☐
☐
☐
☐
☐
☐
☐
☐
☐
☐
☐
☐
☐
☐
☐
☐
☐

COMMENTS: _____

A Daily Planner

DATE:

THINGS TO DO:

Schedule

time	task

COMMENTS: _____

A Daily Planner

DATE:

THINGS TO DO:

Schedule

time	task

COMMENTS: _____

A Daily Planner

DATE:

THINGS TO DO:

Schedule

time	task

COMMENTS:

A Daily Planner

DATE:

Schedule

time	task

THINGS TO DO:

☐
☐
☐
☐
☐
☐
☐
☐
☐
☐
☐
☐
☐
☐
☐
☐
☐
☐
☐
☐
☐
☐

COMMENTS: _____

A Daily Planner

DATE: _____

THINGS TO DO:

Schedule

time	task

- _____ ☐
- _____ ☐
- _____ ☐
- _____ ☐
- _____ ☐
- _____ ☐
- _____ ☐
- _____ ☐
- _____ ☐
- _____ ☐
- _____ ☐
- _____ ☐
- _____ ☐
- _____ ☐
- _____ ☐
- _____ ☐
- _____ ☐
- _____ ☐
- _____ ☐
- _____ ☐
- _____ ☐

COMMENTS: _____

A Daily Planner

DATE:

THINGS TO DO:

Schedule

time	task

COMMENTS:

A Daily Planner

DATE:

THINGS TO DO:

Schedule

time	task

COMMENTS: _____

A Daily Planner

DATE:

THINGS TO DO:

Schedule

time	task

COMMENTS: _____

A Daily Planner

DATE:

THINGS TO DO:

Schedule

time	task

COMMENTS: _____

A Daily Planner

DATE: _____

THINGS TO DO:

Schedule

time	task

- _____ ☐
- _____ ☐
- _____ ☐
- _____ ☐
- _____ ☐
- _____ ☐
- _____ ☐
- _____ ☐
- _____ ☐
- _____ ☐
- _____ ☐
- _____ ☐
- _____ ☐
- _____ ☐
- _____ ☐
- _____ ☐
- _____ ☐
- _____ ☐
- _____ ☐
- _____ ☐
- _____ ☐
- _____ ☐

COMMENTS: _____

A Daily Planner

DATE:

THINGS TO DO:

Schedule

time	task

COMMENTS: _____

A Daily Planner

DATE:

THINGS TO DO:

Schedule

time	task

COMMENTS:

A Daily Planner

DATE:

THINGS TO DO:

Schedule

time	task

COMMENTS: _____

A Daily Planner

DATE:

THINGS TO DO:

Schedule

time	task

COMMENTS: _____

A Daily Planner

DATE:

THINGS TO DO:

Schedule

time	task

☐
☐
☐
☐
☐
☐
☐
☐
☐
☐
☐
☐
☐
☐
☐
☐
☐
☐
☐
☐
☐
☐

COMMENTS: _____

A Daily Planner

DATE:

THINGS TO DO:

Schedule

time	task

☐
☐
☐
☐
☐
☐
☐
☐
☐
☐
☐
☐
☐
☐
☐
☐
☐
☐
☐
☐
☐
☐

COMMENTS: _____

A Daily Planner

DATE:

THINGS TO DO:

Schedule

time	task

COMMENTS:

A Daily Planner

DATE:

THINGS TO DO:

Schedule

time	task

COMMENTS:

A Daily Planner

DATE:

THINGS TO DO:

Schedule

time	task

COMMENTS: _____

A Daily Planner

DATE:

THINGS TO DO:

Schedule

time	task

COMMENTS: _____

A Daily Planner

DATE:

THINGS TO DO:

Schedule

time	task

COMMENTS:

A Daily Planner

DATE:

THINGS TO DO:

Schedule

time	task

COMMENTS: _____

A Daily Planner

DATE:

THINGS TO DO:

Schedule

time	task

COMMENTS: _____

A Daily Planner

DATE:

THINGS TO DO:

Schedule

time	task

☐
☐
☐
☐
☐
☐
☐
☐
☐
☐
☐
☐
☐
☐
☐
☐
☐
☐
☐
☐
☐
☐

COMMENTS: _____

A Daily Planner

DATE:

THINGS TO DO:

Schedule

time	task

☐
☐
☐
☐
☐
☐
☐
☐
☐
☐
☐
☐
☐
☐
☐
☐
☐
☐
☐
☐

COMMENTS: _____

A Daily Planner

DATE:

THINGS TO DO:

Schedule

time	task

COMMENTS: _____

A Daily Planner

DATE:

THINGS TO DO:

Schedule

time	task

COMMENTS: _____

A Daily Planner

DATE:

THINGS TO DO:

Schedule

time	task

☐
☐
☐
☐
☐
☐
☐
☐
☐
☐
☐
☐
☐
☐
☐
☐
☐
☐
☐
☐
☐
☐
☐

COMMENTS: _____

A Daily PLANNer

DATE:

THINGS TO DO:

Schedule

time	task

COMMENTS:

A Daily Planner

DATE:

THINGS TO DO:

Schedule

time	task

COMMENTS:

A Daily Planner

DATE:

THINGS TO DO:

Schedule

time	task

COMMENTS: _____

A Daily Planner

DATE:

THINGS TO DO:

Schedule

time	task

COMMENTS: _____

A Daily Planner

DATE:

THINGS TO DO:

Schedule

time	task

COMMENTS: _____

A Daily Planner

DATE:

THINGS TO DO:

Schedule

time	task

COMMENTS: _____

A Daily Planner

DATE:

THINGS TO DO:

Schedule

time	task

COMMENTS: _____

A Daily Planner

DATE:

THINGS TO DO:

Schedule

time	task

COMMENTS: _____

A Daily Planner

DATE: _____

THINGS TO DO:

Schedule

time	task

COMMENTS: _____

A Daily Planner

DATE:

THINGS TO DO:

Schedule

time	task

COMMENTS: _____

www.ingramcontent.com/pod-product-compliance
Lightning Source LLC
Chambersburg PA
CBHW080720290626
47170CB00017B/2866